The Secret to Writing an Essay:

A Parent's Guide for Teens and Tweens Who Hate to Write

Micheal Maxwell

Dedication

For

Jerry White,

who taught me The Five Ws and the H

and

Dennis Brennan, whose red editing pencil

taught me more about writing

than all my years of college.

Acknowledgement

A special thanks to Megan Boyd without whom this book would never have gotten published.

My wife Janet, faithful and constant sounding board, proofreader, and critic.

Juozapas Pilkakailis for his wonderful illustrations!

Table of Contents

Introduction

Thank you for buying this book. Now, take a deep breath.

I have dealt with at risk, struggling students for more than twenty years. If there is one thing I have learned it is that somewhere along the line, they missed something. Sometimes it was the fault of their environment, family situations, frequent moves, or any of a jillion social ills. It may have been one bad teacher who, was abusive, condescending, or just a lousy teacher. Believe me it happens.

More often or not, it was something long forgotten, perfectly innocent, but just as devastating. Missing a week of school due to the chicken pox, a death in the family and a trip to the funeral, moving to a new school, ditching school for a long weekend at Disneyland, or any of a jillion other normal all-American facts of life.

Fact #1 There is nothing we can do about the past.

Fact #2 We all can benefit from loving guidance.

Fact#3 This book will give you simple steps to take, to lovingly, simply, and effectively overcome the holes in your or (I know there are those of you who bought this book for yourselves) your child, or student's understanding, and that writing and reading are repairable and not the enemy.

Now, exhale. We can do this. With patience (God help us) and understanding that baby steps lead to walking, that eventually lead to running. At times the information may seem simplistic, but it may be the brick in the wall of what was missed way back when, that will finishes things off and brings everything into focus. (Did I just mix a metaphor?)

Remember, you are re-building something that was neglected for years.

I believe in you, and you must believe in your child or student!

Micheal Maxwell

Chapter 1
How I Survived English Class (And Your Kid Can Too)

In the fall of 1970 I entered college. I recall my disappointment at not scoring high enough on the entrance exam to be placed in English 101. Even though I had been in what we now call "College Prep" classes, I found myself missing whatever skills they were looking for to place me somewhere besides "Bonehead English." So for a whole semester I read stories from an expensive anthology and wrote silly little papers for a woman who felt she was imparting some holy knowledge to the thirty or so of us in the class. My papers came back with lots of red lines and circles, none of which were ever addressed in the class. I got a "B."

The next semester I finally landed in the English 101 class and thought, "OK, now I'm really in college." To my amazement, when I entered the classroom printed on my schedule, the lights were out and there didn't appear to be any furniture in the room. In the center of the room burned an oddly shaped candle and three sticks of incense that sat on a brass tray atop a twelve-inch wooden cube.

As my eyes adjusted to the dim light I saw that my fellow students sat along the walls, their faces made ghoulish and sallow by the glow of the candlelight. I took a spot on the wall and waited. Several minutes later the door opened and a man came in carrying a cassette player. As he turned to find an electrical plug, I saw that he had a ponytail tied with a wide black ribbon and wore a denim vest decorated with what appeared to be hand embroidered stars and rainbows. In the center of the vest was a large smiling sun.

He introduced himself as Phillip. He asked us to close our eyes, listen to the sounds on the tape, and use our minds to push any negative energy from the room. Phillip pushed the button on the tape player and the sounds of ocean waves and a creaking boat filled the room. After about five minutes he said, "beautiful" and turned off the tape.

There was no syllabus and no text. We weren't to "get hung up by the menopausal rules and head games put on us by the administration." Phillip explained that writing was communication. Reading was taking in part of the soul of another. Our goal was to be able to write things that people could relate to and to share our soul. We weren't to worry about spelling, grammar, structure, or anything like that. Content was key. Our class was a safe harbor from the negative energy outside the door.

So we spent a semester listening to Phillip read short pieces from books that "turned him on" and lots of poetry, mostly his. We wrote things that we felt expressed our reaction to what he read. One person received great praise from Phillip for having the insight and courage to simply write the word "yellow" in the center of a sheet of paper after hearing a newspaper piece he read about how a corporation controlled of a community of miners.

At the end of the semester Phillip told us all what an amazing journey we had taken him on and how honored he was that we had guided him closer to his center of energy. We were instructed to take out paper, write our names and the grades we wanted, and hand them in. That was our final. I got an A.

Fast-forward twenty years. I find myself sitting in an auditorium full of teachers. On the stage is a small woman in a stylish suit. She is explaining to us how to guide our students' writing. She wants us to really commit ourselves to making sure nothing is left to chance and the structured format she is showing us must be used by every student.

The woman in the stylish suit drew circles and squares and triangles on the whiteboard at the center of the stage. These shapes would help our students bring out responses to the prompts given by using the developed syntax and a rubric that met predetermined criteria that she would provide in the packet we were given. Writing, she said, "was a process that should be structured around preordained standards and expectations".

If you found that last paragraph confusing, you're not alone. Education is a swamp of clever jargon, number crunchers, and the latest legislative agenda for the schools systems across the state and nation to re-tool for. Kids face endless bubble tests every spring and never really understand the whys and wherefores. It is no surprise that some of the more artistically inclined students choose to use the Scantron answer sheet bubbles to recreate the Metallica logo. The old threat of "this will go into your permanent record" no longer carries much weight.

I have worked with "at risk" kids for over twenty years. Frankly, I am sick of that title and sick of what our education system has done to our kids.

Gangs, poor attendance, chemical dependency or abuse, lack of parental control or interest, pregnancy past or present, fatherhood, hunger, isolation because of sexual orientation, fear, obesity, acne, dress or plain old garden variety shyness hold kids back from getting the most out of their educations. Then throw in a myriad of racial, social, and economic factors and you have the world's largest dysfunctional family. Or simply put, today's high school. On second thought it just sounds like the world outside of school, doesn't it?

Let's get one BIG thing out of the way before we start. Your child faces stress, electronic distractions, social media pressures, temptations to do things you have taught them were wrong since the cradle, and the unrealistic goals the education system places on administrators, teachers and your child. ALL THIS DIDN'T EXIST WHEN YOU WERE A KID!

So put aside the "When I was in high school…" mentality because that place only survives in your dusty old yearbooks, memories, and class reunions.

You are holding this book because your son or daughter is in trouble. Your child needs to be able to write to get a decent grade. The most important thing he has going for him is you! What I am going to do is give you some tools that can help him learn to write. You held the back of his bicycle seat when he learned to ride. It's time to give him the same love and support you did then.

Maybe you fear that you aren't the right person to help your child. Maybe you made less-than-super grades when you were in school. Maybe the red marks on your child's papers give you flashbacks of harsh things said about your abilities in the past. So what. You don't need to love Shakespeare or know how to use a semicolon to help your child. What you do need is stuff you already have: love, patience, a willingness to work hard, and the few simple tools contained in this book. You are the best person to help your child because you care the most. Period.

If you are reading this book, you are probably at your wits' end, but so is your kid. It's time for a non-judgmental, heart to heart, "I love you more than anything" tears and hugs conversation. Yelling, arguing, pleading, and teacher conferences haven't worked. News flash: they never will.

If you read my bio, you know I am a successful writer. I was a lousy student in high school. I didn't do homework, I goofed off and was more interested in girls, laughs, and music than what those old fuddy-duddies in front of the room were saying. All of it was a defense mechanism that I used to cover up the fact that I didn't get what they were trying to teach me.

The things I will share with you in this book were taught to me by people who cared enough to turn my thoughts into words on a page that made sense. Odds are your child is not stupid. Same odds he's not Einstein either. Somewhere in the middle is a kid who just needs some tools that make sense and that he can understand.

Sound like anybody you know?

Chapter 2

Busting the Myths That Haunt High Schools

There are a lot of myths that have longer shelf life that a package of Twinkies.

Myth 1 - Everybody's going to college!

Myth 2 - You know you're getting a great education if you can ace a test.

Myth 3 - Writing is a gift. You either have it or you don't.

Myth 4 - You have to be perfect.

This fearsome foursome has shackled and handicapped a lot of good kids (and parents) who, if left alone, would probably have been just fine and a whole lot less frustrated. Let's bust these myths!

Myth 1 - Everybody's going to college!

The availability of a college education in America is the envy of the whole world. We have the best colleges and the best instructors on the planet. Every year thousands come from every country on earth to benefit from our colleges. That does not mean that every butt that fills a seat in a high school will later occupy a seat at a college.

The students who go to four-year colleges and universities are a small percentage of the graduating class of any high school. The number who actually graduate from college is even fewer. The number of high school graduates who enroll in community colleges, on the other hand, is tremendous. The percentage of those enrolled a year later, however, is sadly low. In the end, the majority of high school graduates enter the work force without a college degree.

So, if you are the parent of a normal, average kid who's probably not college-bound, what is your job? Simple: prepare your kid for the real world.

Myth 2 - You know you're getting a great education if you can ace a test.

Having spent the majority of my adult life in the "real world" before becoming a teacher, I know one truth: There are no tests in the real world. OK, driving test and urine tests (one you can study for, the other you can't), but most of life is nothing like a test where you have to have a bunch of facts memorized. Life is an essay. Organized thinking and clear communication count for a lot.

So what do all those tests in school really show us? They show us that information was memorized for long enough to pass a test. That's it. If we are truthful, none of us remember a thing from the statistics midterm we crammed so hard to pass. Education guru, Benjamin Bloom identifies "Knowledge, observation, and recall of information" as the lowest rung on the learning ladder. That means students aren't rising above that level simply because multiple-choice questions are based solely on recall and regurgitation.

We evaluate students on bubbles filled in during times of stress and anxiety. They are asked to recall and repeat only what was presented to them. It's a poor way of finding out what they have really learned.

The ability of students to consider, evaluate, and draw conclusions on any lesson presented to them should be our goal. The fact that Abraham Lincoln split rails, read law, was President, waged war, freed slaves, and was finally assassinated means little if the student cannot connect the dots to his ability to govern through adversity and his strength to hold onto convictions no matter what. Lincoln's deeds mean little if his life doesn't show the possibilities in us all. Rising to our greatest potential no matter what is the legacy left by the sixteenth President. That legacy is much, much more than the sum total of the facts of his life.

The same holds true of almost any lesson. What is the real-life value of the knowledge? The accumulation of facts is fine, but without application, what's the point? If indeed many of our kids join the work force after high school, what can we give them that will be of real value? Being a life-long learner is not about stacks of paperbacks bought at the "Friends of the Library Sale", although that's not a bad thing. Life-long learning is acquiring knowledge that has value and application. If you can take what you learn and apply it to a real life situation, that says a lot more about how educated you are than whether or not you can guess if the answer is A, B, C, or "all of the above."

Myth 3 - Writing is a gift. You either have it or you don't.

I am not an athlete nor do I follow or enjoy watching sports, (I just lost half my readers there, I bet), but I do know that all great coaches have understood the importance of mastering the fundamentals.

Sure, some kids out there seem to have the gift of writing, but it's not because they were born with it. They just mastered the fundamentals early. Maybe they read a lot when they were younger, or someone helped them outside of school. Whatever the reason, their early success has absolutely nothing to do with your child's chance at success now. Anyone who learns the fundamentals of writing can do just fine. You don't have to be a genius.

Let's take inventory. Can your child outline the main ideas in a chapter of their text? Can she write a coherent paragraph communicating what she found that she did not know in the assigned reading? Can she write a short essay on the main concepts of the chapter? Does she know how to pull together the information necessary to do the assignments mentioned here?

If the answer is yes, close the book and pass it on to a neighbor, relative or somebody at work whose kid could use some encouragement and help. If the answer is no then the solution lies ahead.

Myth 4 - You have to be perfect.

Time for a confession. I am a bad speller. Does that mean I can't learn? Of course not. Does it mean I'm stupid? Well that's debatable. Does it mean I won't be a success? Not at all. What does it mean, really? It means that I'm a bad speller, no more and no less. Thank God we now have spell-checkers. Spelling, penmanship, and grammar are kind of like icing on a cake. Please realize, essays don't have to be "perfect" to get the job done. Like Woody Allen said, 80% percent of life is just showing up." 80% is a B. I'll take it.

Wouldn't you love a big red "C" at the top of your child's essay instead of an "F" on her report card because she didn't turn the essay in?

Instead of stressing out about the icing, let's get the cake right. Let's worry about the student's ability to think in an organized way. The ability to solve problems and find answers is so much more important than nice handwriting. The other problem areas can be ironed out with maturity, practice, desire to improve, as well as the motivation born of success.

What you want to look for is the improvement over time of your child's ability to read and understand text and then show that understanding in writing. If your child is asked to write a five paragraph essay explaining the "three main causes of the Civil War" that has a *thesis statement*, clear factual information, and a summary that brings it all together and ties it with a bow, do you really care if a few words are misspelled? If your child understands the key points of the Civil War unit and can give the teacher evidence she understands the material, isn't that what's really important?

Looking to the future, if your kid isn't going to a four-year college right out of high school, what should our real priorities be? I believe that students will do whatever is requested of them in the classroom so long as they find it reasonable. Giving them the tools to write essays (or long answer paragraphs on tests) equips them to do battle. Will they get wounded with a few red marks for spelling or punctuation? Probably, but they are in the battle instead of turning in a blank page like a white flag of surrender, because they didn't know where to start. They have shown up, and shown their willingness to try. Let's go for the big picture (LIFE) and not worry about the little stuff that will come with time.

Now that we've busted a few myths, let's look at one last idea that is NOT a myth.

Not a Myth: 80% of life is showing up.

Students with poor attendance are a big part of the "at risk" community. Here today, gone tomorrow! We teachers often tease students that they are on the three-day plan. Some attend as little as once a week.

The greatest strain on a child's education is not being present. The frustration of "being lost" often results in the student shutting down. Furthermore, missing chunks of what is done in the classroom greatly diminishes the student's ability to receive instruction that builds toward the very writing assignments we are here to improve.

If you have a habitual truant or non-attender for whatever reason, start with baby steps. Double their time at school. Absent two days a week? Six days a month? Cut it in half. Even a small improvement in attendance can result in academic improvement. Work on the other half as their self-esteem and success increases.

Beyond academics, consider that "real world" we agreed you were going to prepare your child for. What real world job allows you to be absent half of the time? The simple habit of getting up every day and getting to where you're supposed to be, whether it's work or school, is one of the best real world habits you can help your child practice today.

Chapter 3

Shushing the Inner Voices That Nag Your Kid

Time for a little tough love. You are the adult. You are the first and, in the end, the only real teacher your child truly needs. In your heart, you know what I mean. I learned from my father until the day he died. Your child learns from you, too.

In this section, I hit some painful truths. Not all apply to your child directly, but please take them in. Someone is influencing your child; it could be someone sitting next to him in class, or a friend that hangs out at your house, if the message is wrong we need to help change it. To fix a problem we must admit there is a problem and that takes understanding the problem. Please remember this book is for you, not your child. We are filling your toolbox to help build your child up, not tear him down.

Your child may have some beliefs or concerns inside himself that are getting in the way of his success. It is a sad but true fact that by the time a student reaches high school a lot of damage has already been done.

"I'm worthless."

Your child may have had harsh or heartless teachers who believed he was dumb, a jerk, didn't care, or a whole list of other untrue deficiencies. Even if it wasn't said aloud, your child probably got the memo loud and clear. Especially if this happened when he was young, he may have spent many years thinking that those red marks on his homework or the failing grades on his report card were a message about his value as a human being. He might feel worthless.

You know that's wrong. You know he's worth so much more than a grade or a test or a teacher's opinion. Tell him that. Make sure he knows that you, his first teacher, believe he is a valuable person no matter what.

"It's just too hard!"

We teachers hear these words all the time. Students say that they hate writing, or that writing is too hard. Like curse words spouted during a moment of road-rage, these are words said in frustration. When people are frustrated, angry, and losing their cool, they say things they don't mean. You've probably done it yourself. I know I have.

If this sounds like your child, take a moment to think about how you respond. My advice is, don't be a fire-and-brimstone preacher who shouts back at her about how she needs to fix her bad attitude and clean up her act. If your child is already frustrated, this is only going to make things worse. Instead, be a calm and level-headed guide who helps her change her frustration into the positive energy she needs to improve.

"It's too hard" and "I hate this!" are just perceptions that come from looking at the situation through anger. Writing is not "too hard." It's a simple job that requires a few tools. Making pancakes is not hard, but try making them without a griddle and a spatula and anyone would get frustrated. Your child may not realize she's just lacking a tool or two. You are the adult. Use your wisdom, your patience, and your life experience to help her perceive the situation in a different way. She may be frustrated, but you can guide her through it. With the right tools and some practice, this frustration is something she can handle, not something that will defeat her.

"It's hopeless."

Every year I have students who begin senior year with less than 25 credits when it takes 200 to graduate (even at an "alternative" site). There is nothing that can be done to get them a diploma by June. They know it, and I know it, but there they are, class after class, just the same. If this is your child, he may feel school is hopeless. If he's been at it for years and is still far from graduating, what's the point? The point is, school can give him more than just a diploma. In school your child can learn lessons he can apply in real life.

Writing is a real-world skill he will need in the job market.

The tools in this book can help him get the most out of his classes at school as well as helping him in life after school. We are a written-media driven society. Companies, business, trade schools, even online colleges are relying more and more on employee and student communication. Learning online, writing email reports on production, equipment problems, and even employees writing their own job evaluations are becoming commonplace.

School is not hopeless if it can be used to acquire and practice skills needed for the rest of life.

"When will I ever need to know this stuff?"

This isn't just the outburst of a smart-mouth kid in the back row. It is a legitimate question that is seldom addressed in a serious manner. In the nearly forty years since it was presented to me, I have never had occasion to solve $(x-x1)2 = r2$ in any configuration. Granted, I *was* that smart-mouth in the back row, but, my question was a real concern of mine and was blown off by the teacher.

There is the need for the acquisition of knowledge as a foundation for future learning. Some things need to be learned just for the sake of carrying on cultural and societal continuity. I am in no way suggesting that all subject matter needs to be justified to the student. However, it is the right of the learner to wonder why the lesson has value. I'm sure there was at least one person in my math class that needed to know how to figure the dimensions of a circle. We need to realize that the practical application of learning will carry it farther than some hackneyed cliché about knowledge being power.

Let's be honest. There are many facts and formulas taught in high school that your child may never use again. What she *will* use again (and again and again) are the character traits she develops tackling challenging work in high school. Hard work is a chance to practice being a hard-working person. A confusing lesson is an opportunity to practice taking responsibility for her learning, asking questions, and not giving up until she really understands. Long and boring assignments help her develop stamina and determination. I doubt anyone has every regretted time spent becoming a determined, responsible, and hard-working person.

Writing is like exercise: the more we do it, the better we get. The assignments in class are like the weight machine used to get stronger. Or, if you've haven't made it to the gym recently (or ever) think of essays and paragraphs like learning scales on a piano, chords on a guitar, or the first few levels on a video game: they have to be mastered to play the instrument or beat the game.

For our immediate purposes we must begin to instill the value of the assignment as a means for practicing the skill of written communication. Frankly, I hate Shakespeare (yes, I said it), but that did not excuse me in college from writing the assigned papers on the Bard. I learned to use hated topics or assignments as a means of proving to myself that I could BS the teacher enough through my structure and writing skill to pass the assignment.

You must teach your child to lay claim to this attitude: I may not love the topic, but I can use my tools to present enough information in an orderly fashion, to earn a passing score. Notice I said "enough!" Not a doctoral dissertation, but enough to pass.

Chapter 4
Get Organized (With An Outline!)

As a first year teacher, I had a student named Ramon in an Adult-Education English class. I learned something from him that changed the way I thought and the way I taught my class from that day forward.

Up until that time, I taught the class with a literature-based curriculum. We would examine a short story or read a short section of a play from our text, answer a few study questions, and then take a quiz or write a short paper. This was the tried and true method I sat through in high school and college and what I was taught to do in my teacher credential program.

One day Ramon arrived to class looking like his best friend had just died. When I questioned Ramon on why he seemed so glum, he gave me the following explanation…

"My boss wants a report explaining why my crew is twenty-five percent slower than the rest of the company. If I don't have it on his desk by quitting time tomorrow, I will lose my job as line foreman."

In my best academic swagger I responded with, "So, what's the problem?" I was amazed to discover that Ramon knew exactly what the problem was. He had all the facts he needed to respond to his boss, BUT he didn't know how to begin because the idea of writing about it terrified him. So we tackled the problem as a class, one step at a time.

Step One: Brainstorm

Believe me when I say, I didn't do anything special. I asked Ramon to tell us (out loud, instead of in writing) why his team was behind in production. I listened, and I wrote on the board what I heard him say. That's all a brainstorm is. Think or talk about the topic. Write it down.

After asking a couple of questions and listening to Ramon's answers, I was able to write on the board three main points:

- The machine is old and breaks down a lot

- It causes delays in production

- It needs to be repaired or replaced

Ramon had the facts he needed to respond to his boss. What he lacked were the tools to organize those facts, and communicate them clearly.

The problem was, no one ever taught Ramon or, as it turned out, the rest of the class, a simple means of gathering thoughts and communicating them. In fairness to the English teachers of the world, the lesson may have been given some time or another, but it was lost in the swamp of grammar, vocabulary, syntax, theme, and plot. Quick write drills may have been on the overhead for years, but were they effective in a real world application? In Ramon's case, he didn't get the connection with the real world.

From that day, until this, it has been my mission to give people the basic tools needed to communicate. The very first tool, before a pen even touches a piece of paper, is brainstorming. Brainstorming can be done alone by writing a list, or it can be done with someone else by simply talking about your thoughts. Discuss or list the facts you know or ideas you have that you think relate to what you're trying communicate.

Let's look at a real world communication-bugaboo that just about everyone faces at some point: the dreaded cover letter. Imagine a young woman (I'll call her Kim) who wants to apply for a job looking after kids at an after school program. Kim knows she's perfect for this job, but she almost doesn't even apply because she's required to submit a cover letter. Just the idea of writing a cover letter causes her anxiety and nasty flashbacks of papers bleeding red ink. Kim knows why she would be great at this job, and she has skills the job requires. What she's missing is the tools to communicate clearly and the know-how to get started.

Let's help her out. Her cover letter should start with a brainstorm. Why should this program hire her? Maybe she would list the following:

- I like working with kids.

- I come up with fun things to do when I babysit.

- I have experience taking care of kids.

- I'm nice.

- I know what to do in emergencies.

- I am responsible.

- Kids usually like me.

Her next step is to choose her best three ideas. She should choose the three ideas that she thinks the employer would care about most. If some of her ideas are similar to each other, she can combine them, or save one to use as a detail to support one of the best three. Kim decides her best three are:

1. I like working with kids.

2. I have experience taking care of kids.

3. I am responsible.

Like Ramon, Kim has used the knowledge she already had, and came up with a few clear and organized thoughts to communicate. Now when she sits down to write her cover letter she won't get lost down a rabbit-trail of unrelated ideas that will just confuse her future employer. She's made a plan about what to communicate and she knows she can stick to it.

Step Two: Outline

In order to turn three main points into an outline, a little detail must be added. Here's how I helped Ramon to expand each of his points:

A) The machine is old and breaks down a lot.

1) It's the oldest machine in the plant.

2) It broke six times in the last 30 days.

3) It's getting harder to find parts.

B) It causes delays in production.

1) We can't meet production if the machine is down.

2) Our crew was 25% behind the rest of the plant.

3) It is very difficult without overtime, which is not allowed.

C) It needs to be repaired or replaced.

1) The machine needs a complete overhaul.

2) The temporary repairs aren't working.

3) The machine needs to be replaced. It will save money.

There's no real magic to figuring out what details to list underneath each of the three main points. I just asked Ramon to "tell me more about that" for each one. Just say a little more about each of the main points and write down about three more things that relate to it. Notice I said they must relate. The 1, 2, and 3 details underneath point A must relate to point A. They should be on the same topic and they should support what point A is saying. Since Ramon's point A is "The machine is old and breaks down a lot," a detail underneath point A should NOT talk about his crew or overtime rules or his suggestions for improving productivity. All the details underneath A need to be about the machine being old and breaking. That's it. Stay on topic!

The same goes for all three main points (A, B, and C). "Say more about that," for each one. Write down three details that support each point (label them 1, 2, and 3 to stay organized). Double-check that each supporting detail is actually related to the point it's supporting. If it's not related, either get rid of it or move it underneath the point it is related to.

Let's go through the same process for Kim's cover letter. Here are her three main points:

A) I like working with kids.

B) I have experience taking care of kids.

C) I am responsible.

Here's how she might say more about each one.

A) I like working with kids.

1) I enjoy kids of all ages.

2) I like coming up with fun games and activities for them.

3) Kids usually like me, so we get along well.

B) I have experience taking care of kids.

1) I have been a babysitter since I was twelve.

2) I take care of my nephews every weekend.

3) I can provide references from three different families I have babysat for.

C) I am responsible.

1) I would get to work on time.

2) I would follow the rules.

3) I know the kids' safety is the most important thing.

Next, she must double-check that all her details are on topic. The 1, 2, and 3 details under point A are all about how she likes working with kids. The 1, 2, and 3 details under point B are all about her experience. The 1, 2, and 3 details under point C are all about being responsible. Nothing is off-topic.

Just like Ramon, her organized outline guarantees that her final essay (or letter) will make sense. As long as Kim and Ramon stick to their outlines, they should have no problem communicating their messages clearly. And in their cases, clear communication means more than a passing grade. It means the difference between real-world employment and unemployment.

Quick note: There are outline templates in the back of this book that you or your child can copy. Please make use of them for organizing thoughts and preparing to write.

Chapter 5

From Outline to Essay

A clear outline is really only two steps away from a decent, passable essay. Each of the main points (A, B, and C) becomes its own paragraph. The 1, 2, and 3 details say what information to write in each paragraph. Once the three paragraphs are written, it's time for an introduction paragraph and a conclusion paragraph and the essay is finished!

Step Three: Three Main Paragraphs

In the outline created in class, Ramon has plenty of *organized* information to begin writing a message to his boss. Here's how he can translate his detailed outline into the paragraphs of his letter:

A) The machine is old and breaks down a lot.

    1) It's the oldest machine in the plant.

    2) It broke six times in the last 30 days.

    3) It's getting harder to find parts.

Becomes…

    The main problem for my crew is that our machine is old and it breaks down a lot. It is the oldest machine in the plant. In the last month it has broken down six times. The parts are getting harder to find and it leaves us waiting for parts to arrive.

B) It causes delays in production.

    1) We can't meet production if the machine is down.

    2) Our crew was 25% behind the rest of the plant.

    3) It is very difficult without overtime, which is not allowed.

Becomes…

    I realize delays in production are a big problem. Obviously we can't meet production with our machine down. We are currently 25% behind the other lines because of breakdowns. Since overtime is not allowed, it is very difficult for us to catch up.

C) It needs to be repaired or replaced.

    1) The machine needs a complete overhaul.

    2) The temporary repairs aren't working.

    3) The machine needs to be replaced. It will save money.

Becomes…

    The only solution to our problem is to either repair or replace the old machine. The machine needs a complete overhaul because of its age. The temporary repairs just aren't fixing problem. The machine needs to be replaced with a new one. This will save the company money in the long run.

Ta-da! We have addressed the problem and offered a solution! These are all solid, well-constructed paragraphs. They're not fancy. They're not long. They don't have big words. Really, these paragraphs say barely any more than was already said in the outline. That's the beauty of it. Once you've got a good outline, the essay is not very far away. Just take the main points and supporting details in the outline and rewrite them in paragraph form. Nothing extra is needed. No distractions, no wandering ideas. Just the basic ideas, simply stated, and well-supported with a few details. That's clear communication.

Same thing for Kim. Now that she's got the outline written she'd be a fool not to apply for this job. Her cover letter is as good as written. Going from outline to paragraphs is as simple as this:

A) I like working with kids.

    1) I enjoy kids of all ages.

    2) I like coming up with fun games and activities for them.

    3) Kids usually like me, so we get along well.

Becomes…

I think I would make a good After Care Assistant because I really enjoy working with kids. I like kids of all ages from preschool to middle school. I can be creative and come up with games and activities for them. I have a fun and silly personality that kids usually get along with really well. I think I will have no trouble relating to and having fun with the kids in your program.

B) I have experience taking care of kids.

    1) I have been a babysitter since I was twelve.

2) I take care of my nephews every weekend.

3) I can provide references from three different families I have babysat for.

Becomes…

I have a lot of experience taking care of kids. Since I was twelve, I have been a babysitter for kids in my neighborhood. I have two nephews who are eight and six, and I take care of them every weekend while my sister works. I can provide references from three different families whose children I have cared for.

C) I am responsible.

1) I would get to work on time.

2) I would follow the rules.

3) I know the kids' safety is the most important thing.

Becomes…

I would be a responsible employee. I would make sure I always got to work on time. I would learn the program's rules and make sure I followed them. I would make sure the kids followed the rules too. I know that the safety of the children is number one so I would never let them do anything dangerous or against the rules.

Just like Ramon, Kim doesn't need any fancy language or complicated sentences. As long as she sticks to her outline, her letter will communicate her message clearly.

Step Four: Introduction and Conclusion

All we are missing from these two almost-complete pieces of writing are introductions and conclusions. My strategy is to go back to the three main points (the A, B, and C in the outline) to help write the introduction and conclusion (or, as I like to call them, the Intro and Outro).

Let's tackle the Intro first.

Tips for Writing an Intro
• State your purpose.
• Include your three main ideas (A, B, and C).
• Directly answer the question or prompt.
• Tell your readers what you're going to tell them.

Let me show what I mean using Ramon's message.

For Ramon's intro paragraph he starts by stating his purpose: explain the problem with production. His bossed asked him to do this, so his purpose was basically given to him. He had to respond to his boss's question. After stating his purpose, he states his three main points (A, B, C) in slightly different words. Here's his Intro:

I would like to explain the problem with our production. The machine my crew works on is old and breaks down a lot. These breakdowns cause delays. This old machine needs to be repaired or replaced. Here are the facts.

Now we're ready to examine the Outro.

Tips for Writing an Outro
• Tell your readers what you told them. • Include your three main ideas (A, B, and C) again but re-word them and switch the order. • Your last sentence should remind readers of your purpose.

Since Ramon's purpose is addressing a problem, his conclusion paragraph (or Outro) should restate his main points and emphasize his proposed solution as well as his purpose. Although the information is really similar to the information in the introduction, he uses slightly different words and the emphasis is a little different.

Here's his outro:

My crew works hard and does not like getting behind. Our old machine breaks down all the time. The repairs take a lot of time. It would save a lot of time and money if the machine was just replaced. I hope this explains why our production is behind.

This insurmountable problem in Ramon's eyes was just like the ones your child faces in English, History and other classes all the time. "Where do I start, what do I say?" It becomes a lot easier with when you have the tools.

Kim can use the same tools to finish off her cover letter. Her intro should state her purpose (applying for the job), and give a preview of her three main points.

Like this:

I am interested in applying for the job of After Care Assistant with your program. I am someone who loves to work with children. I have valuable experience. I know what it means to be a responsible employee. Here's a little more information about me.

Kim's outro should review the same points in slightly different words and emphasize the outcome she's hoping for (getting an interview for this job).

I hope you agree that I would be good at the job of After Care Assistant. I would love the chance to work with the kids in your program. I am experienced and have good references. I am responsible and can do the job. Please let me know if you would like me to come in for an interview. I am excited to get started!

Can you imagine if Kim had let her fear of writing scare her away from applying for this job? It happens all the time, but it doesn't need to happen. With a few simple tools, we've gone through the steps to create two very respectable pieces of writing.

Let's look at the finished outlines and essays as complete pieces.

Ramon's Outline:

A) The machine is old and breaks down a lot.

　　1) It's the oldest machine in the plant.

2) It broke six times in the last 30 days.

3) It's getting harder to find parts.

B) It causes delays in production.

1) We can't meet production if the machine is down.

2) Our crew was 25% behind the rest of the plant.

3) It is very difficult without overtime, which is not allowed.

C) It needs to be repaired or replaced.

1) The machine needs a complete overhaul.

2) The temporary repairs aren't working.

3) The machine needs to be replaced. It will save money.

Ramon's message to his boss:

I would like to explain the problem with our production. The machine my crew works on is old and breaks down a lot. These breakdowns cause delays. This old machine needs to be repaired or replaced. Here are the facts.

The main problem for my crew is our machine is worn out and breaks down all the time. It is the oldest machine in the plant. In the last month it has broken down six times. The parts are getting harder to find and it leaves us waiting for parts to arrive.

I realize delays in production are a big problem. Obviously we can't meet production with our machine down. We are currently 25% behind the other lines because of breakdowns. Since overtime is not allowed it is very difficult for us to catch up.

The only solution to our problem is to either repair or replace the old machine. The machine needs a complete overhaul because of its age. The temporary repairs are just aren't fixing problem. The machine needs to be replaced with a new one. This will save the company money in the long run.

My crew works hard and does not like getting behind. Our old machine breaks down all the time. The repairs take a lot of time. It would save a lot of time and money if the machine was just replaced. I hope this explains why our production is behind.

Kim's Outline:

A) I like working with kids.

1) I enjoy kids of all ages.

2) I like coming up with fun games and activities for them.

3) Kids usually like me so we get along well.

B) I have experience taking care of kids.

1) I have been a babysitter since I was twelve.

2) I take care of my nephews every weekend.

3) I can provide references from three different families I have babysat for.

C) I am responsible.

    1) I would get to work on time.

    2) I would follow the rules.

    3) I know the kids' safety is the most important thing.

Kim's Final Cover Letter:

Dear Hiring Manager:

I am interested in applying for the job of After Care Assistant with your program. I am someone who loves to work with children. I have valuable experience. I know what it means to be a responsible employee. Here's a little more information about me.

I think I would make a good After Care Assistant because I really enjoy working with kids. I like kids of all ages from preschool to middle school. I can be creative and come up with games and activities for them. I have a fun and silly personality that kids usually get along with really well. I think I will have no trouble relating to and having fun with the kids in your program.

I have a lot of experience taking care of kids. Since I was twelve, I have been a babysitter for kids in my neighborhood. I have two nephews who are eight and six, and I take care of them every weekend while my sister works. I can provide references from three different families whose children I have cared for.

I would be a responsible employee. I would make sure I always got to work on time. I would learn the program's rules and make sure I followed them. I would make sure the kids followed the rules too. I know that the safety of the children is number one so I would never let them do anything dangerous or against the rules.

I hope you agree that I would be good at the job of After Care Assistant. I would love the chance to work with the kids in your program. I am experienced and have good references. I am responsible and can do the job. Please let me know if you would like me to come in for an interview. I am excited to get started!

Sincerely,

Kimberly Jones

I hope at this point you agree with me that your child, no matter what teachers, report cards, and red pens have said in the past, CAN WRITE essays that are just as good as the two examples above. It will take work and practice with the new tools, but this is not beyond the ability of your normal, average student who happens to be failing English because of hang-ups and a lack of tools.

Chapter 6
Reading (And Understanding) Fiction

When I was a kid I could run, jump, kick a ball, roll, tumble, or climb the ladder on the slide all day long. If I did any of that stuff today I would A) probably puke my guts out, B) collapse a lung, C) die of complete cardiac arrest spread eagle on the grass, D) all of the above. We all know what it means to be out-of-shape physically. It is just as possible to be out-of-shape mentally.

I wish I had a dollar for every time I have heard a high school student say, "I hate to read." If I hate to exercise I'm not going to do it and I will get flabby and out of shape. If I hate to read I will avoid it at all costs and the process of reading will become exhausting, nausea-inducing torture. The more a person "hates to read," the less he reads. The less he reads, the harder reading becomes. The harder reading becomes, the more he hates it. It's a nasty cycle. If your child is trapped in this cycle, it may be destroying his opportunities to learn. Just like you would do anything you could to save him from other life destroying bad influences, you must help him get out of the "I hate reading" trap.

The flabby, out-of-shape body can be whipped into shape by getting out on the track, into the gym, or onto a bike. For a flabby reader to tone up, he has got to read. Just like the blubber butt on the couch with a bowl of chips and a 64-ounce Big Gulp of Dr. Pepper, he has to get up and get going. Easier said than done, you say. Maybe so. But let's look back at when reading was fun.

As mundane as "See Spot Run" was, it was about a dog. Kids love dogs. Horton hatching that egg was funny, and it rhymed. The silliness of the story, and the anticipation of waiting for the next rhyming couplet kept the young reader engaged and interested. You're right, your child is probably too old to want to read Dr. Seuss, but they are not too old to revisit favorites from Jr. High.

The flabby fifty-year-old doesn't run two miles his first day of trying to get back in shape. Likewise, the high school junior doesn't pick up an eleven hundred page Stephen King novel to buff up their reading skills. Maybe something like *Where the Red Fern Grows* made a connection in the seventh grade. Start off with light weights and build up to benching three hundred pounds.

Please encourage your child to read every single day. Even fifteen minutes of reading, practiced daily, can do wonders for academic confidence and improvement. This might seem unrealistic, but it's not impossible. Here are a few tips that might help make it easier:

> • Be a role model. Whether it's mystery novels, news magazines, or the latest best-sellers, let your child see you enjoying reading. Talk with him about what you read and offer to share it.

> • Ask your child what he is reading for school and you read it too. You might discover some classic novels you missed out on when you were younger, or you might learn new information about science or history. Reading the same material as your child can open the door to interesting family conversations, as well as keeping your child accountable for completing his reading in a non-judgmental way.

> • Encourage your child to read to a younger sibling, cousin, or neighbor. This will benefit them both. Your high school age child can read aloud a chapter book that is too hard for the young child to read alone, but plenty easy for the high school student. Reading to a young child is not embarrassing and it will foster a positive relationship between the two.

> • Go to the library together. Ask a librarian for suggestions. Check out a variety of books. When the books are due, go back and get some more.

> • Think of reading as an entertainment option that can be enjoyed alone or together just live television, movies, or video games.

Remember though, be a guide, not a preacher. The worst thing you could do is introduce a new reading regime and explain how good it is going to be for your child. Reading should be relaxing. Even the hardcore, anti-school hooligan in his heart of hearts knows that reading is important. Somewhere along the line he got derailed, distracted, or depressed about reading and shut down. A quiet, non-threatening opportunity to read is a way back in. Nobody knows how hard it is. Nobody hears the mistakes. But just like the lonely jogger on the road at five in the morning, it is a place to have a knock-down argument with your inner self and prove you can do it.

Let reading something enjoyable and low-pressure, at home, for pure pleasure, be an open door for your child.

Strategies for Reading and Understanding Fiction

I hope your child gets in the habit of reading every day and reading for enjoyment. In the meantime, however, she's still going to have assigned reading for school. Novels and plays assigned in high school English class often get a bad reputation for being confusing, boring, or requiring mind-reading capabilities to just magically know how your teacher wants you to interpret them. Admittedly, all of these things are problems sometimes, but remember, even with a boring assignment from an impossible teacher, your child can still practice those life-long character traits of hard-work and not giving up. Along the way, she might also discover that some of the novels and plays assigned in high school are actually pretty interesting.

If your child is having a hard time understanding the fiction reading assigned for her English class, I have a study guide that can help. It is an active reading study guide, which means that the student must *actively* write on it *while reading.* That means reading will probably need to be done sitting at a desk or table with the book AND paper and pencil. Curling up in bed or soaking in the bathtub while reading a good book is great, but that's for books the reader has no trouble understanding. Go ahead and curl up with the just-for-fun mystery book from the library (you guys did go to the library and get just-for-fun books like I suggested, right?). But, when tackling a school assignment that is challenging to understand, or that is almost definitely going to be followed by an essay or a test, that is the time for writing while reading.

As your child reads, she can increase her understanding by filling out the fiction study guide found in the back of this book. Print and make copies of it, or just copy out the same information into a notebook. As she reads she needs to actively look for, and make notes about the following:

Setting: When and where does the story take place? The answers might be given specifically with the name of a city and a year, or they might be more general like "medieval times, England" or "present day, a small town in the U.S." If the setting changes (because the characters travel or time passes) make note of that, too.

Context: Context means what was going on in history or society in the place and time of the story that might have some relevance. You can almost always get this information *from your English teacher* when he or she talks about the book in class. Here are some examples of possible contexts: The Civil Rights Movement, The Cold War, The Great Depression, The Dust Bowl, The Great Migration etc. Find out and write down the context of the story. And if the context is "The Dust Bowl" and your child has no idea what "The Dust Bowl" is, then she needs to find that out and write it down too. No living in ignorance of a story's context when two minutes on the internet can reveal at least some basic information about that context.

Problems: What problems are encountered in the story? These don't have to be complicated. Frequently, they're not. Even if they seem straight forward, write them down. Understanding the problems in a story can be very important to understanding the story itself because one of the most common structures used in fiction is a problem followed by a solution to that problem.

Plot: Plot is just the English class word for "what happens in a story." For each chapter you read, keep track of anything important that happened or that the characters did.

Characters: It would be almost impossible for me to put too much emphasis on the importance of characters to understanding fiction. At the simplest level, characters are just the people in the story. For all major characters, you should notice and write down their names, ages, whether they're male or female, and any other basic facts given such as their job or their relationship to the main character. At a slightly more complex level, however, you need to also notice characters' traits (Kind? Smart? Mean? Brave? Rude?) AND what actions or other information in the story tells you about those traits. Also, keep a look out for anything a character WANTS. Motivation is the fancy English class term for this. Understanding what a character wants (To get a job? To get the girl? To get back home?) can go a long way toward helping you understand why he does what he does, and ultimately, what is happening in the story. Don't under estimate the importance of characters' traits and wants! They are what makes fiction interesting and what can help make it easier to understand.

Let's take a look at some sample notes using my Fiction Note-Taking Template (found in the back of this book).

Title: To Kill A Mockingbird	Author: Harper Lee

Reading Assignment: Chapter 1

Setting: Maycomb, Alabama 1930s Summer

Context: Segregation, The Great Depression

Problems:	Plot (What Happens):
The kids are afraid of a creepy guy who lives in their neighborhood.	The kids meet a new kid in the neighborhood. The new kid dares Jem to touch the porch of the creepy Radley house. Jem does it.

Characters		
Name and Basic Info	Traits and Wants	How I Know (Evidence)
Scout 5 year old girl	Smart Tomboy	She can already read Plays outside with her older brother, gets in trouble
Jem 10 year old boy Scout's brother	Brave	Never turned down a dare
Dill 6 year old boy new kid in town	Mischievous	Starts the idea of getting Boo Radley to come out

These notes come from the first chapter of the famous (often assigned in English class) novel, *To Kill a Mockingbird.* A couple of comments about these notes:

In the first chapter of *To Kill a Mockingbird,* it doesn't come right out and say the year or the town and state they live in. You might be able to figure it out from some clues, but if you didn't figure it out, it would be just fine to write that it's in the South in the U.S. and that it seems like sometime in the past because their life seems kind of old-fashioned. That's plenty to understand the first chapter. Just pay attention and later when you get that information (in another chapter, or from your English teacher, write it down!

Context is another thing that's not said straight up in the first chapter. There are some clues that segregation and the Great Depression might be relevant, but information about context will usually come from outside your book. If the book is assigned for English class, I would bet money your English teacher's going to tell you the context in class. But, if you are truly on your own to figure it out, the internet can tell you a lot. You can read about the novel itself, the life of the author, the time in which it was published or the time in which the story takes place as well as what else was going on at that time and place in history and you can probably figure it out.

Please keep in mind, the notes don't have to be perfect! They are just the ideas of one reader who paid attention and tried to understand what was read in chapter one. Different readers might have different ideas about which characters or events were "major" enough in the given chapter to be written down. That's okay. As long as your child is reading and writing down his best guess about what's important then that's a lot better than reading and not understanding (and way better than not reading at all).

It might seem like a lot of work to keep notes like this on every chapter. But, really? Is it worse than the stress and panic involved in trying to complete an assignment or study for a test about a book you didn't read or didn't understand? It's just a few sentences and bullet points for each chapter. If it's completed *while reading* it will save time in the future that would otherwise be spent thumbing through the book looking for answers to homework questions.

Remember, there are a lot of things in life you can't control, and your child can't either. You can't control what's happened in the past, or which teacher or what assignment you get. You can't control your natural abilities or God-given talents. But, there's plenty you *can* control. You can control your attitude, your effort, how hard you work, the strategies you try, and how long you stick with something before giving up. Taking notes while reading fiction assignments is a choice your child can make to take control of his reading comprehension.

Chapter 7
Reading (And Understanding) Non-Fiction

Much of the reading your child is assigned for school is not fiction. Much of it will be non-fiction textbooks for history class or science class. Reading *and understanding* these assignments is essential to her success in those classes.

Just like for fiction, if she's not currently completing the reading assignments, that's step one. More frequent, regular reading practice will help make that easier. But in addition to doing the reading, she might also need some tools to help her really understand what's being said and what she's supposed to learn from it. The tools used for understanding fiction (setting, context, characters, etc.) won't help here. But there are plenty of tools and strategies that can help.

Below are a few of my best strategies. All these strategies have one thing in common with my fiction recommendations: they require writing *while* reading. If it hasn't happened already, your child needs to get in the habit of reading with a book AND a pencil and paper. In the back of this book you'll find sample templates for non-fiction note-taking while reading. You or your child can print and make copies of these, but a regular notebook will work just fine as well.

Strategy One: Identify the Main Ideas

Nearly all textbooks are broken up into chapters AND smaller sub-sections within the chapters. Each sub-section is usually given its own heading, which should give you an idea of the topic of the paragraph or paragraphs that follow.

For this strategy, begin by identifying how many sub-sections are within the reading assignment. You can recognize the sub-sections because their headings are usually in bold print or some other kind of noticeable type. For each sub-section: (1) read the section, (2) write one sentence telling the *main idea* of that section.

Let's look at a sample passage of history text your child might be assigned to read to see how this would work.

The French and Indian War

Before anyone in the British colonies was thinking about a war for independence, the colonists were involved in another war on American soil. The French and Indian War was fought from 1754 to 1763. The British and the French competed for control of land and resources in The New World. Various Native American (or American Indian) tribes allied with each side depending upon which European power they believed would best protect their interests. The French and Indian War was costly and long. Great Britain went into debt in order to pay for the war. To repay the debt, the King of England decided to increase taxes on the colonies in America. Ultimately, the colonies' resentment of the new taxes was one of the important factors that led them to seek independence from Great Britain and start the Revolutionary War.

Okay, so what was the main idea of that passage? If you said, "The French and Indian

War," you're not alone (but you're not right either). I can't tell you how many kids (and adults) think that the main idea and the topic are the same thing. The topic is often given in the bold-print sub-heading. It is sometimes just one word or a short phrase. It is what the section is "about" in a way, but there's not enough to it. One word or phrase isn't enough to be a main idea.

I like to tell my students that a main idea is both the "what" (the topic) AND the "what about it." A main idea should be a sentence that says something about the topic. Let's start with a simpler example than the French and Indian War. Imagine that the topic of a paragraph is "dogs." Depending on what's said in the paragraph, the main idea could be so many different things. The main idea could be "Dogs make good pets for families," or "Dogs can be trained to assist blind people," or "Dogs are closely related to wolves." These three would be extremely different paragraphs! "Dogs" alone is not enough to be the main idea of a passage. "Dogs" could be the "what," but the "what about it" is needed in order to complete the main idea.

So going back to our passage about the French and Indian War, we already have the "what" (The French and Indian War), but we still need the "what about it". Go back and reread it to see if you can answer: What is this passage telling us about the French and Indian War?

In this case, both the first and the last sentences give us clues. This paragraph is telling us something about how The French and Indian War relates to the Revolutionary War. Specifically, the passage is telling us that the French and Indian War was one of the *causes* of the Revolutionary War. While the paragraph does give some basic facts about the French and Indian War, it focuses on the facts that led to increased taxes from Great Britain, caused resentment among the colonists, and caused the colonists to demand independence and start the Revolutionary War. While there is probably more than one right way to state the main idea of this passage, it should be something like, "The French and Indian War was one of the causes that led to the Revolutionary War."

Identifying the main idea of a sub-section in a textbook is an important step toward making sure you understand it. If your child can't tell in her own words what a passage is trying to say, or at least attempt to write a one-sentence main idea for that passage, chances are she didn't understand what she read. If that's the case, my advice is to aim for a smaller goal first. Can she restate in her own words what one sentence is trying to say? Okay, how about the next sentence? If she can put the meaning of each sentence correctly in her own words, then she should be pretty close to being able to state the main idea of the paragraph.

If your child is a very out-of-shape reader, this sentence-level restating may be necessary to practice for a while before she can jump straight to identifying the paragraph's main idea. Starting with one sentence really is okay if that's what's needed. Think of it like those early push-ups on your knees before you can move on to push-ups on your toes. If you practice knee push-ups consistently, soon enough you'll have built the muscle for toe push-ups and won't need to do knee push-ups anymore.

If your child's assigned reading was a chapter that included three different sub-sections of text, then her notes on the chapter should have three one-sentence main ideas. Here's an example of how that might look:

Chapter 8: Events Leading Up to the American Revolution

A) The French and Indian War was one of the causes that led to the Revolutionary War.

B) New taxes and other laws made the American colonists angry.

C) American colonists wanted representation in the British government.

Strategy Two: Be a Reporter

Everyone knows the job of a news reporter is to investigate a story and tell the public the important facts: Who, What, Where, When, Why and How. This is also an excellent strategy for understanding non-fiction text. After my students had completed the assigned reading and identified the main idea of each section, I would ask them to use this reporter's technique as the next step in their study process.

Answering these "Five Ws and the H" questions can help a student further his understanding by completing the picture in his mind. If you can say what's happening, when and where it's happening, who's doing it, and why and how they're doing what they're doing, you probably have a pretty good understanding of the situation.

Let's apply the reporter's method to the next sub-section of our chapter on the events leading up to the American Revolution.

Intolerable Acts!

Hoping to pay back the debt acquired to pay for the French and Indian War, the British Parliament passed The Stamp Act in 1765. This was a direct tax on the American colonies and required that almost all printed material such as newspapers and legal documents be printed on specially stamped paper produced in London. The Stamp Act, along with other new laws known as The Townshend Acts (1767), and The Intolerable Acts (1774), made the American colonists angry. The colonists viewed these new taxes and laws as harsh and unfair burdens placed on them by a government far away on the other side of the Atlantic Ocean. The American colonists protested, but Great Britain would not budge.

Who: British Parliament and the American colonists

What: Disagreed about new taxes and laws

Where: In the American colonies

When: 1760s and 1770s

Why: The British government wanted the money to pay back their debts. The American colonists were angry about the new taxes because they thought they were unfair.

How: It didn't solve the problem, the British wouldn't budge.

When using the reporter's technique, make sure you pay close attention to the "why". Names, dates, and places really only get you so far. Understanding the motivations behind the actions is much more important to really "getting" what's going on (especially when studying history). Look in the text for clues about what the people involved wanted as well as any emotions (like angry or jealous). These can be big hints about why they did what they did.

Strategy Three: Make An Outline

Yep, you read that right, another outline. I really can't overstate how helpful these are. While making an outline for your essay can help you organize your thoughts before writing. Making an outline as you read can help you make sense of the organization that's already there. Generally, textbooks are pretty well-organized, but if the reader doesn't notice the organization then a huge key to understanding is lost. Making an outline as you read forces you to tune-in to the existing organization and logic of a chapter. Recording that outline in your notebook also gives you a great study aid at test time.

To make an outline, your child should go back to the list of main ideas created earlier on. The outline is simply, the main ideas listed (as A, B, C) with supporting details listed underneath each letter (as 1, 2, 3). Let's take a look at one more sample passage.

No Taxation Without Representation

Leaders and thinkers in the American colonies discussed what to do in response to the high taxes they believed were so unfair. One big idea emerged from these discussions. The taxes were unfair because the American colonists had no representation in the British Parliament. Therefore, they were required to pay without ever getting to vote on what the tax would be. Colonial leaders like Samuel Adams and Patrick Henry helped to spread this idea and convince other colonists that they should not agree to be taxed if the colonies were not permitted representatives in Parliament. "No Taxation Without Representation" was their rallying cry. Soon, many others agreed with them and would not back down. With neither the British government nor the American colonists willing to compromise, war was on the horizon.

To create an outline based on this passage, begin with the main idea:

C) American colonists wanted representation in the British government.

Then, reread the passage and add at least three details provided in the passage that support this main idea, like this:

1) American colonists had no representatives in the British government

2) Samuel Adams and Patrick Henry thought that taxation without representation was unfair

3) They convinced others to agree with them and fight the British

Once your child has completed an outline for all sub-sections of her reading, the outline itself should tell the story and make a great reference for future studying. A completed outline for the chapter "Events Leading Up the the American Revolution" might look like this:

A) The French and Indian War was one of the causes that led to the Revolutionary War.

1) British and French fought over control of the New World.

2) The war was costly and Great Britain went into debt.

3) The King of England raised taxes on the American colonies to help pay the debt.

B) New taxes and other laws made the American colonists angry.

1) The British Parliament passed the Stamp Act (a tax on printed materials) and other new laws.

2) The American colonists thought the new laws were unfair.

3) The colonists protested the new laws.

C) American colonists wanted representation in the British government.

1) American colonists had no representatives in the British government.

2) Samuel Adams and Patrick Henry thought that taxation without representation was unfair.

3) They convinced others to agree with them and fight the British.

The Three-Day Study Plan

Just like with fiction, my recommended approach to reading and note-taking might seem like a lot of work. On the other hand, if it results in better understanding and acceptable work with passing grades, isn't that worth it? Putting in the hard work to follow a study plan is something that your child CAN do. It doesn't involve any wishing and hoping for miracles. It simply requires that your child sit down and do the work.

For what it's worth, here's the plan I recommend for reading *and understanding* a chapter of a textbook.

Day 1:

    Read the chapter.

    Write down the chapter's title and the sub-headings.

    For each sub-heading, write down the main idea.

Day 2:

    Reread the chapter. For each sub-heading, write down the Who, What, Where, When, Why and How.

Day 3:

    Reread the chapter.

    For each main idea written down on Day 1, write down three supporting details to create an ABC123 outline.

If your child completes all three of these steps to the best of his ability, I can assure you, his understanding of the material will be much better at the end of Day 3 than if he had just read (or pretended to read) the chapter one time. If this chapter is followed by an essay or a test on the material, he will certainly perform better on that as well.

Chapter 8

Cooking Up an Essay for English Class

I'll admit, we've gotten off-course a little bit from our original focus: writing. I don't regret the detour, because I hope I've been able to convince you of the importance of reading (and understanding what's read). Writing and reading go hand in hand. It may be impossible to improve on one without improving on the other at the same time.

While some writing assignments or real life communication challenges may only draw on information already in the writer's head, the majority of school writing assignments are going to draw on new information that has recently been presented in class or presented through reading. The reason is, a writing assignment is a pretty good tool for measuring someone's understanding. If a person can write a logical and organized response on a given topic then they probably understand that topic pretty well. So, when teachers want to check if a student understands what was read or taught, assigning an essay is one of the main ways they do it.

In this chapter, we'll tackle essays assigned for English class that are designed to measure a student's understanding of some work of fiction. In the next chapter, we'll look at some essays that might be assigned to measure understanding in other subject areas.

Common Essay Recipes

Okay, so let's assume your child has read *and understood* a novel or play assigned for her English class. She wrote while she read and took good notes. She listened in class when her teacher explained the context. Is this enough to write a decent essay? Well, it's pretty close.

I would say all of that is comparable to standing in a clean and well-stocked kitchen, with a full fridge and pantry. She has all the raw materials she needs to make something, but she still needs a plan. To make something good, she probably needs a recipe. Now, I know that there are plenty of great cooks out there that can whip up a meal without a recipe. Maybe you're one of them. But, chances are if you can cook without a recipe that's because you have a lot of practice, skill, and confidence in your cooking. There are great writers who write without plans or recipes too, but they've got lots of practice, skill, and confidence in their writing. If your child was one of these writers, I doubt you'd be reading this book.

Until your child puts in some practice hours and develops her skills and her confidence, she should be writing with a recipe. There's no shame in that. In fact, plenty of excellent cooks (and writers) rely on tried and true recipes long after they could probably do without them, simply because they work. Why mess with a good thing?

So, here are the basic recipes that your child needs to become familiar with:

~Essay Recipes~

1. Support your Point of View

2. Identify the Author's Point of View

3. Cause and Effect

4. Compare and Contrast

Those four are enough to get you through most writing assignments with dignity. Kind of like the ability to make beans n' rice, spaghetti, soup, and scrambled eggs has kept many a single person fed on a slim budget, knowing how to make these basic essay recipes will keep your child alive through high school English and beyond.

We'll test-run two of the recipes in this chapter, using them to display understanding of fiction. In the next chapter we'll try the remaining two recipes on some non-fiction topics.

Support Your Point of View

This is probably the most frequently used essay recipe in existence. If your child only masters one of these recipes, it should be: Support Your Point of View. Almost any essay assignment that is stated as a question can be answered using the "Support Your Point of View" recipe. Let's work through an example.

Assignment: Based on your reading of To Kill a Mockingbird by Harper Lee, what kind of parent is Atticus Finch?

To answer this, your child will need to have read and understood the novel. But assuming he's got that part, what's next? Step one to composing a "Support Your Point of View" essay, is coming up with your point of view. Typically, it is not necessary that "your point of view" (or your answer to the question) be your most deeply-held belief, or even be correct in the teacher's opinion. It just needs to be a possibly correct answer that has some evidence to back it up.

In this case, the question is: What kind of parent is Atticus Finch? Perhaps your child's immediate response would be: He's a good parent. While that's not enough for a whole essay, it's a fine start. Step two, after coming up with your point of view, is to "say a little more about that." What evidence do you have that he is a good parent? The goal here is to come up with three reasons. (Hint: Use the notes taken while reading!). If there aren't three good reasons to support your point of view, you may need to try broadening your point of view or changing it slightly until you can find three good reasons to support it.

Your basic answer to the question will become the main idea of your essay, and your three good reasons for it will each become the main idea of their own paragraph. Like this:

Answer: Atticus Finch is a good parent.

Because:

A) He is caring toward his children.

B) He gives his children good advice.

C) He sets a good example for his children.

Did you notice the old A, B, and C are back? Once you see them, you've got to know that 1, 2, and 3 aren't far behind. You guessed it. Step three is to find evidence in the book that supports each of those ABC main ideas. Find three details that directly support each paragraph's main idea. Once again, those notes taken while reading should come in handy. If one of the main ideas doesn't have enough evidence to support it, you might need to change it. Finding enough supporting detail is key! Don't skimp! AND, don't throw in unrelated stuff. ABC must *directly support* the main idea of the essay. The 1, 2, and 3 supporting details must *directly support* the A, B, or C idea that they are underneath. Interesting ideas about the book that don't directly support one of your main ideas *do not belong in this essay.*

Here's how the outline ought to look after completing step three:

Answer: Atticus Finch is a good parent.

Because:

A) He is caring toward his children.

1) He reads to his children.

2) He's okay with Scout being herself and being a tomboy even when other people say she should be more ladylike.

3) He listens to Scout's side of the story when she has problems at school or a disagreement with her brother.

B) He gives his children good advice.

1) He advises his children not to fight, but to use their minds instead.

2) He says it's best to be honest.

3) He says you'll never understand someone else until you consider things from his point of view.

C. He sets a good example for his children.

1) He is polite to other people no matter what.

2) He doesn't brag about his abilities.

3) By taking Tom Robinson's case, he shows that a person should live by his own conscience, not by popular opinion.

Once the outline is complete, the essay is not far from being finished. Change the outline into sentences and paragraphs, add an intro and an outro, and that's it. The final essay would look something like this:

In the book To Kill a Mockingbird by Harper Lee, Atticus Finch is a good parent. His wife died years ago and he has had to raise his two children, Jem and Scout, on his own. Being a single parent is hard, but Atticus does a good job by caring for his kids, giving them good advice, and setting a good example for them to live by.

An important part of being a good parent is caring about your kids, and Atticus is very caring. He spends time reading to his children. That shows that he loves them and cares about their education. He tells his daughter Scout that he likes her just the way she is even though she's a tomboy. Her aunt thinks she should be more ladylike, but Atticus doesn't think that's important. Atticus also listens to Scout's side of the story. When she gets in trouble or in an argument he always listens to what she has to say about what happened so that she knows he really cares about her.

Dads are known for their words of wisdom, and Atticus has some wisdom to share with his kids. Throughout the book he offers his children good advice. For example, he encourages Jem and Scout not to fight with their fists but to use their minds instead. He reminds his children to be honest even when it's easier to lie. And most importantly, he teaches his children not to judge other people without thinking about things from the other person's point of view first. All of this advice teaches some very valuable lessons that his children can probably use throughout their lives.

Atticus Finch doesn't just talk the talk with good advice, he walks the walk, too. He sets a good example for his children through his own actions. The way he treats rude neighbors and townspeople shows that he believes in being polite to others even if they are impolite to you. When Jem and Scout learn that their dad is known for being a great marksman, they realize that he has never bragged about this ability. He doesn't think bragging is right, so he doesn't do it. One of the most important ways he sets an example, of course, is by agreeing to defend Tom Robinson. This is a very unpopular thing to do, but he does it anyway because he believes a person should live by his conscience, and not worry about popular opinion.

By caring, advising, and setting a good example, Atticus Finch is able to be a good parent to his children. Jem and Scout know that they are loved and cared about. They know they can ask their dad for advice if they get into trouble. And they will be able to model themselves after the good example their father set for them with his life. The character of Atticus Finch shows us that a single parent can have a really valuable influence on his children.

Identify the Author's Point of View

This recipe is pretty similar to "Support Your Point of View." There's still going to be one main answer, three main ideas that support it, and then three details supporting each of the main ideas. The difference is, instead of coming up with an opinion to answer the question, the writer has to think back to what was read and figure out how *the author* would probably answer the question. This doesn't require mind reading. The author wrote a whole book that should give a lot of clues about her opinion on the topic. If your child read the assigned book carefully and *took notes while reading,* then figuring out what the author probably thinks shouldn't be too hard.

Let's look at a sample essay question where your child would want to use the "Identify the Author's Point of View" recipe.

Assignment: Harper Lee grew up in the segregated South before the Civil Rights Movement. After reading her novel To Kill A Mockingbird, do you think she agreed with segregation?

The short answer to this question to this question should be obvious to anyone who has read and understood the book: No. Harper Lee did not agree with segregation. But, given that this is an essay question, it should also be obvious that "No" is not a long enough answer. The key to this recipe is that the writer must not only *identify* the author's point of view, but also support why this must be what the author thinks.

Just like before, the basic answer to the question (No, Harper Lee did not agree with segregation) will become the main idea of the essay. The main idea must then be supported by three good reasons from the book.

Answer: Harper Lee did not agree with segregation.

Because:

    A. Jem and Scout are allowed to spend time with Black people.

    B. Racist attitudes have bad results.

    C. Scout learns that she should not judge people too quickly.

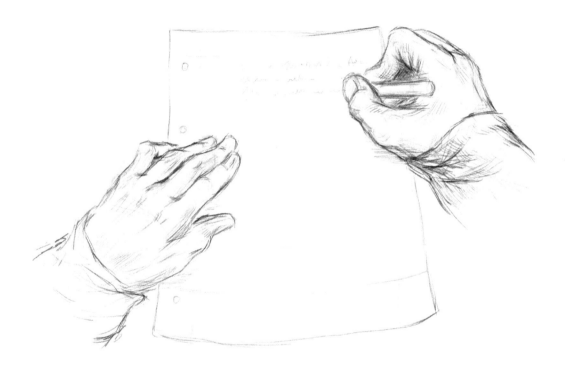

Hopefully this process is starting to feel pretty familiar by now. Just like in cooking, there are certain steps like chopping onions or boiling water that get used again and again in writing. Now that the essay has a main idea and three good reasons supporting it, each of those reasons needs three details for support.

Here's how the outline ought to look:

Answer: Harper Lee did not agree with segregation.

Because:

A. Jem and Scout are allowed to spend time with Black People.

    1. Father trusts Calpurnia to care for them and takes her side in disagreements.

    2. The kids go to a Black church with Calpurnia.

3. During Tom Robinson's trial Scout and Jem sit in the "Colored" balcony.

B. Racist attitudes have bad results.

1. Atticus believes that someday society will have to pay for all the injustice done to Black people.

2. In Maycomb society it is an embarrassment for Tom Robinson, a black man, to feel pity for a white person.

3. It is impossible for Tom Robinson to get a fair trial because of his race.

C. Scout learns that she should not judge people too quickly.

1. Scout wants to be friendly to Walter Cunningham, even though he is looked down on for being poor.

2. Scout feels sorry for Mayella, even though she falsely accuses Tom.

3. People believed that Boo Radley was crazy and scary, but he defended Scout and Jem.

Once again, turn the outline into sentences and paragraphs, add an intro and an outro, and the essay's done. Here's how a completed "Identify the Author's Point of View" essay might look:

Harper Lee grew up in the segregated South, but, based on her book To Kill a Mockingbird, she did not agree that segregation was right. In the book, the main characters cross the race boundaries of their society. There are also many examples of the negative results of racism. One of the important lessons learned by the main character is a lesson against segregation: that people should not be judged by their appearance or first impressions. Harper Lee used the characters and story of her novel to make the point that racism and segregation are wrong.

The Finch family, who are the main characters of the novel, don't follow the town's strict rules about race. For example, Scout's father trusts the word of the family's Black cook, Calpurnia, and will take her side in an argument. This is exactly the opposite of how the townspeople treat the word of Black citizens who are assumed to be lying. Even though Scout and Jem are white, they are taken to visit a Black church and people there welcome them. During the trial of Tom Robinson, Scout and Jem also sit in the Black section of the courtroom. Even though most people in Maycomb would think this was inappropriate, their father says it's okay. Atticus Finch believes Black people are equal to whites, and he tries to teach his children this.

Harper Lee also includes many examples of bad results that racism can have. Atticus Finch talks about how white people often treat Blacks unfairly and he thinks that at some point society will have to answer for this injustice and there will be a debt to pay. Another sad result of race prejudice in Maycomb is that the white people in the town think it's an embarrassment and not acceptable for a Black person to feel sorry for, or show pity toward, a white person, no matter what. Even though Mayella Ewell is poor and abused and has an obviously difficult life, it is not acceptable to most people in Maycomb that Tom Robinson, a Black man, would try to help her or have pity for her because he is supposed to be "beneath" her. Probably the most obvious example of the negative results of racism is Tom Robinson's conviction. He is innocent and he has a good lawyer to defend him, but society is so prejudiced against him because of his race that it's impossible for him to really get a fair trial.

The biggest lesson that Harper Lee includes in her novel is a lesson about not judging people when you don't really know them. The main character, Scout, gets to know many different people in the town who are judged unfairly by others. Scout's classmate Walter Cunningham, for example, is treated unfairly in school because his family is poor. Scout feels this is not right. Later, Scout learns to see past shallow judgments of other people too. Mayella Ewell is clearly lying and it would be easy to think she is just "trash" as some people see it. But Scout learns that Mayella has a sad and hard life and there is more to her story than meets the eye. Scout's neighbor Boo Radley is the best example of someone who gets judged too quickly. In the beginning of the book the children are afraid of him because of rumors that he is crazy and violent. But his actions show another side to him. He actually cares about the children and turns out to be very brave and willing to defend them when they are threatened.

The novel To Kill a Mockingbird shows that Harper Lee was against segregation and thought racism was a big problem in the South. Harper Lee chose to have her main characters break some of the race boundaries in their segregated town. She also used her novel to show the bad effects that racism can have. Scout, the main character, learns an important lesson about not judging people before you get to know more about them. Based on her book, Harper Lee appears to be someone who would disagree with segregation.

A decent "Identify the Author's Point of View" essay has clear support with details from the book. Your child should avoid stating opinions without back-up found in the book, and he should avoid including random other ideas that aren't directly related to the main idea of the essay. If your child can follow the recipe, stay on target, stay organized, and provide support from the book, his essay will earn a passing grade.

Chapter 9

Not-So-Secret Recipes for Essay Success in Every Subject

Knowing how to read, take notes, organize thoughts, and write an essay are skills that will help any student in just about any class. Don't make the mistake of thinking this stuff is limited to English class. It definitely isn't! Organized thinking, careful reading, and thoughtfully planned writing will help your child make it through science classes, history classes, and just about any subject she faces. I can say that I've heard of many essays being assigned in math class, but if they were the strategies in this book would help there too.

In this chapter we're going to test-run two more popular essay recipes. These are recipes that certainly could come up in English class, but we're going to use them for a history assignment and a science assignment just to prove the point that these tools are versatile! The two stand-by recipes we have yet to explore are: Cause & Effect, and Compare & Contrast.

Cause & Effect

"Cause & Effect" is the recipe a writer should whip up whenever the question or assignment asks about a process or a chain reaction. Key words to look for in a question are: cause, effect, affect, result, because, and how. Cause & Effect can come up in English, History, or Science class. Let's take a look at how it might be used to answer a Science class question.

> *Assignment: Describe how heat energy would cause water to change from solid to liquid, and then to a gas.*

Did you catch the key words "how" and "cause"? This question is checking to make sure the student understands a process and can show how and why one thing follows another in that process. The most important thing to get right in the essay is the order of events. The second most important thing to get right is the reason or the "why" for each event. To plan our answer, we'll want to start by writing down the correct order of events in the process.

Answer: Order of Events

    A) Water starts in solid form (ice)

    B) Water changes to liquid form (water)

    C) Water changes to gas form (steam or water vapor)

Notice the "A, B, C"? We're making another outline! Once the basic steps are written down in order, go back and add details under each of the steps. For a Cause & Effect essay, the details should be: descriptions of the step or event plus reasons or the "how & why" of that step. Here's the same outline, expanded with some details:

Answer: Order of Events

A) Water starts in solid form (ice)

1) Water is solid (ice) when below 32 degrees F.

2) The molecules don't move very much.

3) The molecules are packed together in a way that makes it hard to move through them.

B) Water changes to liquid form (water)

1) When enough heat energy is added to ice, the ice melts.

2) The molecules begin to move around more.

3) It is possible to move through them.

C) Water changes to gas form (water vapor)

1) When even more heat energy is added, water begins to evaporate.

2) The molecules move even more.

3) It is even easier to move through the molecules.

To really nail this particular essay recipe, the writer must understand the process or chain of events she's writing about. That's why teachers assign essays, remember? They are checking to see if the student really understands what was taught or read. The Cause & Effect essay is not something your child can fake her way through. If she doesn't actually understand what's being asked, then the problem is happening somewhere before writing the essay. Maybe the problem is with reading and understanding what she read. Or maybe she needs to speak up and ask questions to the teacher when something is not clear in class. Assuming that your child understands the material, however, this essay recipe shouldn't be too difficult.

For the Cause & Effect recipe, don't worry too much about having exactly three main paragraphs (sometimes called "body paragraphs"), or exactly three details under each main idea. In this recipe the number of body paragraphs should be equal to the number of steps in the process. The number of details to describe or explain each step might be a little less or a little more than three, depending on the topic. Just make sure that every step has some detail supporting it, and that no supporting details taught in class are left out.

Once your child has planned out a solid outline, all that is needed is an intro, an outro, and to turn that outline into sentences. Your child can also use a little bit of "special sauce" with this recipe.

Cause & Effect Recipe Special Sauce	
Transition words for the beginnings of paragraphs	First, Second, Third (etc.) Next, Last, Finally
Key phrases to highlight cause & effect and to connect one step to the next	"because of" "as a result" "causes" "leads to" "therefore"

It's definitely not necessary to use every single one of the special sauce words and phrases, but do use at least some. These words and phrases help a reader (teacher who's grading the essay) follow what the writer is saying, and they make the writer sound smart. Look for the special sauce in the following sample essay based on the outline above.

Matter exists in three different forms: solid, liquid, and gases. Adding or subtracting heat energy causes matter to change its form. Water is the most familiar example of matter changing its form, because we can see water in all three states in everyday life.

First, we will look at water as a solid. When the environment is cold, like outside in the winter or inside a freezer, water takes the form of ice. Ice is water that's a solid. It only exists if the temperature is 32 degrees Fahrenheit or less. If you looked at ice under a powerful microscope you would see that the molecules don't move around very much. They are frozen in a crystal structure. This also means that you can't easily move through ice (unless it breaks). That is why it's possible to ice-skate on a frozen pond without falling in.

Next, with a little more heat energy, water will turn to a liquid. Heat energy (from the sun, for example) warms the ice and as a result the ice begins to melt. When the water molecules are heated they begin to move around more and they aren't so rigid. Because the molecules are moving more it is also possible to move through water in its liquid phase. Instead of ice-skating on top of the pond like in cold weather, a person could swim in the pond in warm weather.

Finally, when even more heat energy is added to water the liquid begins turning into a gas. The gas form of water is called water vapor. Water vapor is what makes up clouds and also steam. Sometimes this process happens slowly as heat energy from the sun warms the surface of a pond or puddle on a sunny day. The water molecules begin to move around even faster and therefore change into water vapor (a gas). This is called evaporation and it is the reason that rain puddles eventually dry up. When a lot of heat energy is added all at once (such as if you place a pan of water on the stove), the process happens faster. The liquid water begins to boil and changes into steam. Water vapor is even easier to move through than liquid water. For example, it's not very hard to run through fog (clouds of water vapor near the ground), but it is pretty difficult to run in a swimming pool.

The three phases of matter are easy to see when you consider water in all its forms (ice, water, and water vapor). In everyday life you can observe the differences between them. Adding heat energy causes these differences. The more heat energy is added, the more the molecules move, and the easier it is to move through the substance.

Compare & Contrast

The Compare & Contrast recipe is the last basic recipe your child absolutely must have in his writing cookbook. This recipe can be used for both fiction and non-fiction in almost every class. It's excellent for demonstrating understanding of new material learned in class or through reading. It also has its own special sauce!

Let's first make sure we're all on the same page about the meaning of "Compare &

Contrast." Technically, "compare" is supposed to mean that you tell how two things are alike, and "contrast" is supposed to mean that you tell how two things are different. In reality, though, people often use just the word "compare" to mean both things. So, if your child gets an essay assignment that asks him to compare and contrast two things OR just to compare two things, what the teacher is looking for is an essay that tells how those two things are both alike and different.

Here's a sample question from history class that could be answered using the "Compare & Contrast" recipe:

Assignment: Compare and contrast life in the South versus life in the North before the Civil War.

To best prepare the "Compare & Contrast" essay, I suggest a planning step that comes before the outline. It's sort of like the brainstorming step that Kim had to complete before writing her cover letter. Remember? The "Compare & Contrast" plan can be set up like this:

Life in the South before the Civil War	Both	Life in the North before the Civil War

Make a three-column chart where the two outside columns are for the two things that are supposed to be compared, and the middle column is labeled "both." The outside columns are the place to write down anything that was unique about one or the other, and the middle column is the place to write down anything that they both share. At this point, your child should write down anything he can think of. Later he can go back and pick the best ideas. Remember, this is only possible if your child actually understands the material. If he doesn't know enough about life before the Civil War to fill out this three-column chart then he doesn't know enough to write a passing essay on that topic either. If he's getting tripped up at the planning stage, that means it's time to go back to look at his notes, reread the textbook, or ask the teacher for help.

Assuming he understands the material, here's what his completed planning chart might look like:

Life in the South before the Civil War	Both	Life in the North before the Civil War
Allowed slavery More countryside (rural) Farms Fewer railroads	Part of the United States (governed by state governments, federal government, Constitution) Economy based on producing and selling goods	Mostly did not allow slavery More cities (urban) Factories More railroads

Once the chart is done, your child should pair up the ideas in the two outside columns that relate to one another. In our example the pairs would be:

Allowed slavery < > Mostly did not allow slavery

More countryside (rural) < > More cities (urban)

Farms < > Factories

Fewer railroads < > More railroads

If there are any ideas with no partner on the other side of the chart, then he needs to either come up with the partner idea and add it, or cross out the idea (it may be correct, but it doesn't belong in this essay). If there are more than three pairs of ideas, it's time to narrow it down to three. He can either pick the three he thinks are best, or choose to lump two pairs together because they are related in some way. In our sample list, we have four pairs. Here's how the final list would look with two of those pairs lumped into one pair:

Allowed slavery < > Mostly did not allow slavery

More countryside (rural, farms < > More cities (urban, factories)

Fewer railroads < > More railroads

Once he's got three strong pairs of ideas, he's ready to start making his outline. The three pairs will become the main ideas in the essay's body paragraphs. Don't throw out the ideas in the "both" column just yet. Later, those will get used in the intro and outro paragraphs!

Let's do the outline…

Assignment: Compare and contrast life in the South versus life in the North before the Civil War.

Answer:

A) One difference was whether or not slavery was allowed.

1. Southern states permitted slavery

2. Many Southerners believed slavery was necessary for running their farms

3. Most Northern states did not permit slavery

4. Many Northerners believed that slavery was morally wrong

B) Another difference was the landscape and how people made their living.

    1. The South was very rural

    2. People in the South made their living off of agriculture (farms that grew cotton and food crops)

    3. The North was more urban (it had big cities)

    4. Many Northerners made their living by working in factories

C) A final difference was the transportation that was available.

    1. The Northern cities were connected by railroads

    2. In the South, fewer railroads had been built

    3. This made a big difference in how quickly people as well as goods could be moved

You might have noticed that I didn't stick to exactly three supporting points underneath each main idea here. For this essay recipe, I don't think that it's as important to have exactly three. It is more important to include the important points (even if there are more than three) and leave out the irrelevant stuff (even if that means you end up with less than three). Probably either two, three, or four supporting points would be fine in most cases. If your child is tempted to go crazy and include ten points, he probably needs to cut back. And likewise, a main idea with only one supporting point might not deserve its own paragraph.

Hopefully you haven't forgotten that I promised a special sauce for this recipe too. Once again, the special sauce is made up of words and phrases that can help a reader follow what's being said, and just make the writer sound good.

Compare & Contrast Recipe Special Sauce	
Phrases for the beginnings of paragraphs	"One difference" "Another difference" "A final difference"
Key words and phrases to highlight differences and similarities	"While" "On the other hand" "similar to" "different from"

Just like before, the writer doesn't need to drown the dish in special sauce. No need to include every word and phrase listed above. But, a few of them (used properly) will go a long way toward helping the writer make his point, and helping the reader understand what's being said.

Another bonus with the "Compare & Contrast" recipe is that if the planning is done correctly then the intro and outro are ready-made. The best ideas your child listed in the "both" column during the planning phase will go right into the intro (and outro) along with the statement that "despite these similarities, _____ and _____ had several important differences." Something very similar can be repeated in the outro, just using slightly different words.

As you read the sample essay below, keep an eye out for special sauce words and phrases as well as the ready-made appetizer (intro) and dessert (outro).

Before the Civil War, the South and the North were two very different regions of the same country. Both regions were part of the United States of America. They were governed by a combination of federal and state laws as well as the U.S. Constitution. Both regions' economies were based on producing and selling goods to one another. But, despite these similarities, the pre-Civil War North and South had several important differences. These differences included their laws and beliefs about slavery, their landscapes and jobs, and their methods of transportation.

One difference (probably the most well-known difference) between the North and South was whether or not slavery was allowed. Southern states permitted slavery. People in the south had relied on the labor of enslaved Africans to run Southern farms and plantations for more than two-hundred years by the beginning of the Civil War. Many Southerners believed that slavery was necessary and that their farms would fail without it. On the other hand, the Northern states mostly did not permit slavery. Many Northerners felt slavery was immoral.

Another difference between the North and South at this time was the landscapes and economies of the two regions. While the South was a rural region, the North was more urban. People in the South mostly made their living by farming. They grew cotton as well as food crops and sold it to people in the North and elsewhere. In the big cities of the North there were many more factories than in the South. Many Northern people made their living by manufacturing and selling all kinds of man-made goods.

A final difference between the North and South was the transportation options available in the years before the Civil War. Travel in the South was usually slow. People could travel or transport goods from one town to another using horses. People did travel on horseback or use horse-drawn vehicles in the North as well, but they had another option: railroads. Railroads connecting Northern cities allowed people and goods to be moved much more quickly. While there were some railroads in the South, there weren't as many as in the North and they didn't connect as many places.

Even though the North and the South were part of the same country, the everyday lives of the people were very different. Different opinions about slavery would eventually lead to a big conflict: The Civil War. The two regions different economies, landscapes, and transportation options, would have a big impact on the war.

Chapter 10

The Combined Powers of Love and Spell-Check

I hope I've been able to convince you of the wide-ranging value of basic writing know-how. If your child learns to read for understanding, take organized notes, and write organized essays using the four recipes we've discussed, there is absolutely no reason he can't earn passing grades in English and other subjects as well. The tools I'm offering in this book aren't going to make anyone a genius, but I believe they can help any struggling student to improve.

Finishing Touches

Earlier, I mentioned how grammar, spelling, and punctuation were not that important in comparison to organization of thoughts in writing. I stand by that 100%, but once the organization is in place, there is, of course, something to be gained from cleaning up the details a bit. But please, don't forget these are details. Spelling and punctuation are not writing. If you can spell and punctuate perfectly, but can't form a coherent thought or express yourself in a way others can understand then what's the point? If you can think and write in an organized way, however, correct spelling and punctuation can be the icing on the cake.

Here are some simple tips for adding some final polish to organized, thoughtful writing:

Utilize Technology: Every device from computers to tablets to phones has a spell-check tool on it these days. Many of them have grammar-checks as well. Why not use them? If your word processing program is popping up with little red and green squiggly underlines, don't ignore them. Click to find out what they mean, and make changes if you need to. There's no reason to misspell a word when your computer is one click away from providing you with the correct spelling.

Double Check Sentences: You don't need an English degree to check for complete sentences. A complete sentence *must* have a subject (that's a person, place, thing or idea that the sentence is about), AND a verb (an action that the subject is doing). If either one of these is missing, the sentence is incomplete and needs to be corrected. Here are a couple quick examples to show you what I mean:

Incomplete	Complete
The ball.	The ball rolled down the hill.
The baby.	The baby cried.
Mark Twain.	Mark Twain is a famous author.
Florida.	Florida has warm weather.

In all four of these examples, the sentence must be completed by adding a verb to the subject. Verbs can be really obvious actions like "rolled" or "cried," but they can also be a little less obvious like "is" or "has." Some common but less obvious verbs are: am, is, are, was, were, has, had, and have.

Keep It Simple (Stupid): Though I don't generally go in for name-calling, that old acronym (KISS, or Keep It Simple, Stupid) absolutely applies in writing. I have seen so many struggling writers fall into the trap of trying to make their writing sound smart with fancy, complicated sentences. Trust me, unless you really know what you're doing, fancy, complicated sentences make you sound stupid. They show that you don't know what to do with commas, or you don't know the right way to use those big vocabulary words. Fancying it up is NOT a good strategy. Keep your sentences simple and short and they will sound just fine. In fact, in the business world (especially in the United States) writing with short, simple sentences is *the* way to write.

Check Periods and Capital Letters: Teachers have probably been hammering this into your child's head since he was in second grade. If an eight-year-old can get this right, then your teenager can get this right too. Every sentence must start with a capital letter. Every sentence must end in a period. True, sentences can also end in question marks or exclamation points, but those don't usually show up a lot in essays written for school. There are dozens of rules about how to use commas properly. Even college graduates (even college graduates with English degrees) mess them up half the time. My advice is, don't worry about commas or semi-colons or whether or not to capitalize weird things like "The Middle Ages." Just make sure every sentence has a beginning capital and an ending period. That's enough.

Take It With You

As you finish the last few pages of this book, my hope is that at least a few ideas have stuck and you feel hopeful about your ability to help your child. Kudos to you for picking up this book, for reading it all the way through, and most of all for caring about your child. Love and concern for a child is one of the biggest motivators in a parent's life. It's the reason you work hard at your job, it's the reason you stress out about problems, it's the reason you hold your child to a high standard, and the reason you feel angry if she falls short. You know in your heart how much she is capable of, and you care so much that it is painful to see your child fail. Love for your child is a powerful force. If you take nothing else away from this book, please take with you the belief that the power of love can work wonders. Sorry if that sounds cheesy, but it's true.

Your child needs to build up his confidence and believe in himself. You can help by showing him you believe in him. Your child needs the tools to handle what's asked of him in school. Now that you've read this book, you have some tools you can share with him. Your child needs hope that no matter how bad things look now, they can get better. He may not have lived long enough to know that first-hand, but you have. Share your experience with him. Tell him how hard work and asking for help and refusing to give up have helped you in your life, even when things looked hopeless.

In addition to these positive messages, your child probably also needs help ignoring negative messages. Not all teens have the maturity to do this on their own. You have maturity. When fears and doubts creep in, demonstrate how to confront them and chase them away.

What if your child just isn't smart? So what? Smart isn't everything. Character traits like effort, determination, and doing the right thing mean much, much more than intelligence ever could.

What if the deck is stacked against him because he goes to a bad school, or has a teacher who doesn't like him, or he has English at 8:00 in the morning when he's still half-asleep? Who goes through life without experiencing a stacked deck from time to time? Better to learn how to handle it now when he has a parent to help coach him through it, than later in life when the stakes might be higher and he might be all on his own.

Doubts and fears are natural and normal. You will have them. Your child will have them. I have them. It's how we respond that counts. Don't let them paralyze you or taunt you into giving up. That's what leads to students turning in a blank page and earning a zero when they might have earned a D or C with some effort. Sure, Ds and Cs aren't sending anyone to Harvard, but they're a heck of a lot better than zero.

Thank you for sticking with me long enough to get to the end of this book. Whether or not he says it to you now, your child thanks you, too. You've stuck with him longer than the few hours necessary to read a book, and you will stick with him much longer than that. You are his life-long guide, coach, and teacher. Thank you for doing all that you can for him to pass along the tools, the wisdom, and the strength of character that it takes to face life with dignity.

Like the Rolling Stones said: "You can't always get what you want, but if you try some time, you just might find, you get what you need!"

PLEASE CONSIDER THIS

If you think the ideas in this book will help you and you student take a moment now and leave a review on the site you purchased it. Readers like you are the best advertisement in the world!

Appendix

 The material that follows is provided as an additional tool to reinforce what we have covered in the book. If you are reading this on a Kindle, Nook, iPad or a similar reader, simply copy them onto binder paper. If you are a computer Wiz type them up in Word and hit print! If have the paper version, off to the copy machine you go!

Easy Definitions of Key Words in an Assignment

Analyze: Break the issue or problem into separate parts and discuss, examine, or interpret each part and the relationships between them. Sometimes this involves looking carefully at causes and effects.

Analyze the Argument and the Conclusion: Look at the truth and persuasiveness of the reasons given for a position and the degree to which the conclusion is justified on the basis of those reasons.

Compare and Contrast: Describe the similarities and differences between two objects, situations, or ideas. Sometimes this involves a before-and-after comparison.

Define: Tell what a particular word or term means in your essay. Usually, this is not a dictionary definition; rather, it clarifies the way in which you are using the term.

Describe: Give a detailed account, naming characteristics, parts, or qualities.

Discuss: This is a general term that covers explanations, reasoning, pro and con arguments, examples, analysis, and so forth.

Evaluate: This term literally means to determine the "value" of something, to discover how good or bad something is. It usually means that you should argue that something is good or bad, and then discuss your reasoning.

Explain: Help the reader understand the reasoning behind your position by showing the logical development in step-by-step fashion. You might also be asked to show how something works or how to do something.

Illustrate: In a writing prompt, this usually does not mean to draw pictures. Instead, it means to give examples.

Prove: This usually means that you should support your opinion with facts and arguments.

State: Tell the reader your opinion strongly and concisely.

A_____

B_____

C_____

A

1_____ 4_____

2_____ 5_____

3_____ 6_____

B

1_____ 4_____

2_____ 5_____

3_____ 6_____

C

1_____ 4_____

2_____ 5_____

3_____ 6_____

A_____

B_____

C_____

Fiction Note-Taking Template

Title:	Author:

Reading Assignment:

Setting:

Context:

Problems:	Plot (What Happens):

Characters

Name and Basic Info	Traits and Wants	How I Know (Evidence)

About the Author

Micheal Maxwell was taught the beauty and majesty of the English language by Bob Dylan, Robertson Davies, Charles Dickens and Leonard Cohen.

Micheal Maxwell holds a Master's Degree in Education with a concentration in Curriculum and Instruction from Chapman University in Orange, California. Mystery readers know him as the international bestselling author of the Cole Sage Mystery Series, and the young adult time travel novel, The Time Pedaler. Maxwell lives in Northern California with his wife and traveling partner, Janet. They have three grown children, and three grandchildren.

Micheal Maxwell writes from a life of love, music, film, and literature. He lives in California with his lovely wife and traveling partner, Janet.

Sign up for Micheal's Newsletter and receive a free eBook.

Visit Micheal's Blog !

Become a fan of Micheal on Facebook.

Made in the USA
Columbia, SC
09 December 2023

28122272R00037